# GOLD GLOVES

Doug Marx

The Rourke Corporation, Inc.
Vero Beach, Florida 32964

Copyright 1991 by The Rourke Corporation, Inc.

All rights reserved. No part of this book may be reproduced or utilized in any form or by any means, electronic or mechanical, including photocopying, recording or by any information storage and retrieval system without permission in writing from the publisher.

The Rourke Corporation, Inc.
P.O. Box 3328, Vero Beach, FL  32964

Marx, Doug.
    Gold gloves / by Doug Marx.
      p.cm.—(Baseball heroes)
    Includes bibliographical references (p. 46) and index.
    Summary: Discusses the relative merits and importance of various defensive positions in baseball, including first base, shortstop, and center field, and celebrates great defensive players in the history of the sport.
    ISBN 0-86593-130-5
      1. Baseball—United States—Defense—Juvenile literature. 2. Fielding (Baseball)—Juvenile literature. 3. Baseball players—United States—Biography—Juvenile literature. [1. Baseball—Defense. 2. Fielding (Baseball) 3. Baseball players.]  I. Title.  II. Series.
GV870.M39    1991
796.357'2—dc20                                                                                    91-2225
                                                                                  CIP
                                                                                  AC

Series Editor: Gregory Lee
Editor: Marguerite Aronowitz
Book design and production: The Creative Spark, Capistrano Beach, CA
Cover photograph: Darrell Sandler/SportsLight
Consultant: Zak Colandrea

# Contents

| | |
|---|---|
| Introduction | 5 |
| History | 9 |
| The Pitcher | 13 |
| The Catcher | 17 |
| The First Baseman | 21 |
| The Second Baseman | 25 |
| The Third Baseman | 29 |
| The Shortstop | 33 |
| Outfielders | 37 |
| Conclusion | 44 |
| Glossary | 45 |
| Bibliography | 46 |
| Index | 47 |
| About The Author | 48 |

Chris Sabo

# Introduction

It is late October 1990, and the underdog Cincinnati Reds have just completed an amazing four-game sweep of the powerhouse Oakland Athletics. In years to come, fans will remember the performances of Reds pitcher Jose Rijo, who won the Most Valuable Player award. They will remember Reds outfielder Billy Hatcher's seven consecutive hits and .750 batting average.

But will they also recall Reds third baseman Chris Sabo? Besides helping his team at the plate, he stole run after run from the power-hitting A's with his sparkling infield play. Sabo once told a reporter that his first passion in life is fielding ground balls. In Game Three he proved it, setting a record for most plays in one game—ten—without an error. The Reds' championship was won as much in the field as at the plate. By the same token, bad fielding plagued

*Bo Jackson*

5

*These are just a few of the types of gloves that have been used throughout the years.*

the A's throughout the Series. Costly errors took them out of each game.

**Defense! Defense!**

How many times have you heard a crowd yell DEFENSE! during a football or basketball game? Probably a lot. Nobody questions the importance of defense in these two popular sports, or with many others including volleyball, hockey and soccer. Yet when it comes to baseball, it is the hitters who usually get all the glory.

Pitchers get plenty of attention, too. But how often

do we think of a pitcher as the key defensive player on a team? A pitcher's entire job is to keep runners from getting on base and scoring, which is the best defense. After all, a "perfect game" in baseball is one in which the losing team scores no runs and no runners reach first base.

Defense is one of the most beautiful aspects of baseball. It is as dramatic as a game-winning home run, and just as rewarding to watch. Defense is the world of the running, over-the-head diving catch in the outfield. It is the sneaky pick-off play and the acrobatic double play in the infield. It is a catcher throwing out a speedy base runner trying to steal. It is the close collision-play at the plate when a runner tries to score from second on a bloop single.

Defense is the world of the Gold Glove Award winners, the major-league wizards of the infield and outfield who are voted each year as the best at their position. In the pages that follow, we will celebrate many of these players. We will also talk about the players of olden times, many of whom played the game barehanded! Along the way, we will also discuss the importance of each position and the skills and techniques needed to play them well.

*Hack Wilson of baseball's golden era hauls one in.*

# History

*We used no mattress on our hands,
No cage upon our face;
We stood right up and caught the ball
With courage and with grace.*
—George Ellard

It is hard to imagine baseball's defensive game 100 years ago. The ball was "dead." Because baseballs in those days did not have cork or rubber centers, they did not fly as fast and far as today's baseballs—but they were just as hard. Fielders with broken fingers were just starting to get used to wearing little, stubby gloves—so small they could fit in a hip pocket. Toothless catchers were just starting to use masks and chest protectors. Shin guards would not be introduced until 1908. The pitching distance had just been lengthened to its present-day 60 feet, six inches. Pitchers were beginning to throw overhand— and fast.

But no matter how primitive the equipment, or how many runs were scored, defense was ultimate baseball. This was hard to

**Mel Ott**

believe, however, when in a 1885 playoff game between the National League's Chicago White Stockings and the American Association's St. Louis Browns, the teams made 100 errors between them!

Still, when we think of today's fielding masters, we must recall their respected tradition. Some believe that shortstop Honus "The Flying Dutchman" Wagner, who played for the Pittsburgh Pirates from 1900 to 1917, was the greatest ever—including Ozzie Smith. A contemporary of Wagner, Napoleon "Naps" Lajoie, played second base with the grace and quickness of a cat. His 988 accepted chances (or plays made) in one season with Cleveland stood as an American League record for decades.

We will talk about some of the fine players of yesteryear, position by position, throughout this book. Whether they were as good as today's players remains a matter of friendly argument. However, this much is true. With the introduction of the "live," "jack-rabbit," cork-centered ball in 1910, defense lost its glory and hitting became the name of the game.

In 1957, the Rawlings Sporting Goods Company created the Gold Glove Award. It was the first time in baseball's history that an award was given solely for superb defensive play. In each year since, 18 glove- and mitt-shaped trophies have been presented to the best player at each position in both leagues. The list of the winners is long and legendary.

With the help of the Gold Glove Award, defensive baseball has come into its own. In fact, from the days of pebble-strewn infields to artificial turf, from bare hands to mitts as big as pillows, defensive baseball has entered a golden age.

## Judging

Baseball statistics do not leave much to question when

we talk about hitters and pitchers. For example, the number of home runs, runs batted in (RBIs, or "ribbies," as they are often called) and batting average make it clear who is a good hitter and who is not. For pitchers, a win-loss record can be deceptive, but a low earned run average, or ERA, is proof of real talent.

There are statistics that show a player's hustle. For fielders, judges look at the number of *putouts* made. A putout is scored to the fielder who actually makes the out. Flyouts are putouts. So are tagging a runner and catching the throw for a force-out. Many first basemen make 15,000 putouts in their careers.

With fielders, the statistic used most often is the fielding average, or FA. If, out of 100 attempted putouts or assists, a player makes 95 of them, his FA is .950. Although the FA is the most common way of judging a fielder's performance, it can be unreliable.

For example, compare two shortstops of similar talent. One never hustles and dives, never risks a throw. Playing it "safe," he has a perfect 1.000 FA. The other is a sparkplug ballplayer who goes after everything, misses a few, but overall makes more outs. Which one is better? Willie Mays caught over 7,000 fly balls in his career, which is an all-time high for putouts among outfielders. Yet Mays is not among the all-time, top-ten FA leaders.

Judges also note *assists,* which are usually throws made that result in an out. Infielders make a high number of assists. Of course they have to get to and catch the ball before they can throw it. The number of double plays started or shared is also important for infielders.

These are some of the ways that big-league managers and coaches look at ballplayers when they vote their Gold Glove Award selections.

*Jim Palmer was one of the better fielding pitchers.*

# The Pitcher

**M**any fans think a pitcher's only job is to get the ball over home plate with as much speed, junk and control as he can. The rest of the team is supposed to make the plays and score the runs.

But a good, all-around pitcher will be a good infielder, too. He must have a sneaky pick-off move. He must complete his pitch in a balanced position, ready to field bunts and dribblers to his left or right, and "comebackers," or balls hit up the middle. He must also be prepared to cover first, third and home. And most important, he must be ready to save his life and career! Standing 60 feet, six inches from the plate, a pitcher is in the most dangerous defensive position.

More than one big-league pitcher has had his career ruined by taking a smoking shot to the body. In 1936 the great St. Louis Cardinals pitcher Dizzy Dean had his career shortened when a line drive hit his ankle. In 1957, the career of Herb Score of the Cleveland Indians ended when he was hit in the eye by a hard drive off the bat of New York Yankee Gil McDougal.

Not even great fielding pitchers are safe. Bob Gibson of the St. Louis Cardinals, who won the National League Gold Glove Award nine years straight (1965-73), had his leg smashed when Roberto Clemente ripped a shot up the middle. Fortunately, Gibson's injury healed and he went on to more fantastic years in baseball.

Jim Kaat, who played for the Minnesota Twins and the Chicago White Sox, won the Gold Glove Award 14 years in a row (1962-75), a record for pitchers that

*Bob Gibson's career spanned 17 seasons, and he won nine Gold Gloves.*

might never be broken. Kaat says, "Most of fielding for the pitcher is reflexes. The rest, like getting over to cover the base or backing up on plays, is what you learn to do." Kaat also adds that breaking to first every time a ball is hit to the right side of the infield is a pitcher's first rule.

Of the great fielding pitchers—a list that includes Jim Palmer, Ron Guidry, Phil Niekro and Rick Reuschel —the best was Bobby Shantz. At five-feet-six inches and 130 pounds, the left-handed Shantz *had* to play superb defense, if only to make up for what he lacked in size. During his career Shantz made unheard of plays. One time a high hopper was hit back to the mound. Shantz turned, ran toward second like an outfielder, caught the ball over his head, wheeled and fired to first for the out.

A smart pitcher takes advantage of every opportunity. Shantz demonstrated that defense is as important to a pitcher as a good fastball and curve. In fact, they are inseparable.

*Johnny Bench*

# The Catcher

There have been some all-time great Gold Glove catchers in the last ten years. Gary Carter, Lance Parrish and Bob Boone are three. When fans think of catchers of the past, they talk of Gabby Hartnett, who played for the Cubs from 1922 to 1941. Or they might mention Roy Campanella, who played for the legendary "Boys of Summer" Brooklyn Dodgers of the 1950s. Or the Yankees' lovable Yogi Berra.

The catcher's mitt is extra big, but never as big as the one used by Baltimore Orioles Gus Triandos. Frustrated with trying to catch Hoyt Wilhelm's famous dipsy-doodle knuckleball, Triandos had a special mitt made that was nearly twice as big as his regular one! Imagine what an old-time ballplayer of the 1880s would have thought of that. Pitchers threw just as hard in those days, but catchers' mitts were not much bigger than a child's glove of today.

Ask any fan to name the finest catcher ever, and almost all will agree: Johnny Bench. Bench played with the Cincinnati Reds' "Big Red Machine" of the late 1960s and 1970s. Besides hitting 389 home runs, Bench won the Gold Glove Award ten years in a row, from 1968 to 1977. He modernized the position in at least two ways. He updated the equipment, for example, by introducing the big-pocket, hinged mitt. And he developed new styles of play such as catching the ball one-handed and tagging runners out at the plate like an infielder. A superb athlete, Bench made a dirty, awkward position seem like a glamorous job.

*Benito Santiago is one of today's great catchers.*

A catcher's basic skills involve more than handling burning fastballs and tricky curves in the dirt. He must be quick on his feet, able to gobble up bunts, and have an arm that is strong and accurate. Plus, he has to catch those dizzying, mile-high pop-ups behind the plate.

A catcher must also have a lot of grit and stamina. Physically, catcher is the most grueling, injury-prone position in baseball. Knees and toes weaken from constant squatting. Thumbs and fingers get battered by foul tips. Some catchers put a sponge in their mitts to take the sting out of a fastballer's pitches. Then there is the occasional bone-crunching collision at home.

But most of all, the catcher is the leader and

brains of the team. From his spot behind home, he views the whole field. He is the team's "quarterback." He must know each hitter's weaknesses and his pitcher's strengths. He is his pitcher's best friend and psychologist. He calls the pitches and targets the strike zone. Reminding his teammates of the count and number of outs, he talks to them about strategy pitch by pitch. Though he crouches in foul territory and sees the play "backwards" compared to his teammates, the catcher is always at the center of the game.

*No one played first base better during the 1980s than Keith Hernandez.*

# The First Baseman

There are two outs in the bottom of the ninth, with the tying and go-ahead runners on second and third. A grounder is slashed deep in the hole at short—a sure game-winning single. Amazingly, the shortstop backhands the ball, wheels and hurries a low throw to first. The first baseman, off balance, stretches out like a gymnast doing the splits and digs the ball out of the dirt. Game over. "Great play!" everyone cheers, as the shortstop gets slapped on the back. The shortstop goes to his first baseman and says: "Thanks for making me look good— you're a life saver."

Next to the catcher, the first baseman participates in more plays per game than any other player. This means that the success

---

### Fielder's Trivia

*Q:* What great Yankee first baseman played 2,130 consecutive games, setting one of the most amazing records in the history of professional sports?
*A:* Lou "The Iron Horse" Gehrig.

*Q:* What Dodger catcher—and the first black catcher in the majors—won the Most Valuable Player Award three times?
*A:* Roy "Campy" Campanella.

*Q:* What great Yankee third baseman broke the single-season double play record with 54 when he started out with Cleveland in 1971?
*A:* Graig Nettles.

*A pitcher must be prepared to break toward first base after each throw.*

of the rest of the infield depends on the skill of the first baseman. How many times have you seen a first baseman dig a throw out of the dirt? Or leap for a wide throw, catch it, and tag the runner charging by? Or dive to his right, snag a ground ball, then lob the ball to his pitcher covering the base?

A good first baseman makes the whole team look good. Those wild throws could have been *errors* charged to a teammate. That "blue darter"—a low ground ball hit so hard that it looks like a blue streak—could have been a hit.

George Sisler, who played for the St. Louis Browns in the 1920s, was the finest fielding first baseman of the pre-modern era. He used a little, oval-shaped mitt about the size of a ping-pong paddle. It was all thick padding around a pocket in which the ball fit like a pinball in a socket. It did not have a web—the netting that fills the space between the thumb and forefinger.

There were other magnificent first basemen in the days of yesteryear. Jimmy Foxx of the Boston Red Sox, and New York Yankee Lou "The Iron Horse" Gehrig, for example. Many of today's first basemen are Hall of Fame material. Two of the best are Keith Hernandez and Don Mattingly.

Hernandez is a superior first baseman who has held the Gold Glove Award since 1978. He leads all active first basemen in double plays, and is the all-time first-base leader in assists. He gets to balls that other players cannot touch. His range is so good that the whole infield can shift a bit to its right, better covering the middle and third-base line. More than once he has barehanded a bunt to the *left* side, throwing a runner out at third!

Ryne Sandberg

# The Second Baseman

Second base is the "sleeper" position of the infield. Second basemen are often unfairly thought of as "weak-side" glovemen. They have fewer members in the Hall of Fame than any other position except third. Yet some of the most exciting players of all time have been second basemen, right in the thick of the action.

Among old-timers, Eddie Collins is considered the smartest fielder to have ever played second. Then there is Brooklyn Dodger Jackie Robinson. In 1947, Robinson became the first black man to break the color line in professional sports. A sparkling infielder, magnificent base runner and clutch-hitter, Robinson did it all. Before the late Billy Martin became a feisty big-league manager, he played a feisty second base for the Yankees. His playing days are best remembered by the somersaulting catch he made of Jackie Robinson's infield pop-up, which saved the Yanks' 1952 Series.

Other second basemen have been World Series heroes, too. In the early 1960s, the Pirates' Bill Mazeroski and the Yankees' Bobby Richardson—both long-term Gold Glove winners—led their teams to championships with solid hitting and game-saving defensive plays. Mazeroski is the all-time double play leader.

More recently, the play of Pete Rose and Hall of Famer Rod Carew has proved that second basemen are anything but "sleepy." Though neither received a Gold

*Frank White was one of the premier second basemen of the 1980s.*

Glove Award, they were tough-nosed defensive players who could beat a team three or four different ways. Scrappy, high-percentage slaphitters, daredevil base runners, and diving infielders, Rose and Carew epitomize second basemen.

Among today's second basemen, Ryne Sandberg has been a Gold Glove winner since 1983. Sandberg's American League counterpart, Frank White, is an eight-time winner of the prize.

Talking to baseball author Jim Kaplan, White makes big claims for second basemen. He says that they are "better athletes" than shortstops! White points out the acrobatic difficulties of the double-play pivot. He also points out that second basemen handle the ball more often than shortstops, which is statistically true. They need more range, and cover more ground than shortstops. Moreover, second basemen usually make their plays in awkward, off-balance positions.

No wonder second basemen get annoyed when their feats are overlooked by the Hall of Fame. The list of classic second basemen who have not been voted in is long, including Nellie Fox, Bobby Richardson and Red Schoendienst. Perhaps in the years to come, second basemen will begin to get the recognition they deserve.

*Philadelphia Phillies star third baseman Mike Schmidt won the Gold Glove ten times.*

# The Third Baseman

Baseball fans get into some heated arguments when they start talking about who was "the greatest" at a given position. There have been some great third basemen. In the pre-modern era, Harold "Pie" Traynor made other third-sackers look like amateurs. Since the 1920s, and the introduction of the "live ball," the list of Gold Glove winners is a manager's dream. It includes such gifted ball handlers as brothers Ken and Clete Boyer, Ron Santo, Buddy Bell, Graig Nettles, George Brett and Mike Schmidt—a ten-time Gold Glove recipient.

In fact, one of the most dramatic "match-ups" in the World Series occurred in 1980 between the Royals and the Phillies when Brett and Schmidt played against each other. Defensively *and* offensively, they were the best in their leagues. With the series tied 2-2 and the Royals leading Game Five by one run, Schmidt drilled a liner to Brett's left. Brett dived for it, knocking it down, but he could not throw Schmidt out. Schmidt's hit kept the Phillies in the game. They went on to win the Series, four games to two.

Despite all this talent, the debate dies down when the name Brooks Robinson is mentioned. Robinson played out a 23-year career with the Baltimore Orioles. He is the all-time leader in games played, chances accepted, fielding average, putouts, assists and double plays. He owned the Gold Glove Award from 1960 to 1975.

*Baltimore's Brooks Robinson owned third base—
and the Gold Glove.*

In the 1970 World Series, Robinson's magic destroyed the slugging Cincinnati Reds. He made diving stops to his left and right, fielded bunts and dribblers barehanded, and leapt high to snag line drives. Nicknamed "Hoover" or the "Human Vacuum Cleaner," on one big play Robinson knocked down a hard drive to his right, retrieved the ball 25 feet behind the bag, and still threw the runner out!

Third base is called the "Hot Box." Bullet liners and turf-scorching grounders are routine. Speed is not essential. A strong arm is helpful, but a fast release is better. Reflexes, quickness and brains are more important. Robinson could judge where a ball would be hit before it left the hitter's bat.

Also, a third baseman must be fearless. Hot-boxers

are willing to take anything hit their way, even if that means stopping the ball with their body. Hall of Famer George Kell once took a Joe DiMaggio smash to the jaw. He picked up the ball, crawled to the bag for a force out, and then fainted.

Danger aside, third basemen are the focus of high-stakes drama. They get the pleasure of stealing more extra-base hits from the hitters and preventing more runs than any other fielder. That is their true reward.

*Ozzie Smith*

# The Shortstop

It used to be that shortstops were, literally, short guys who usually hit about .250. In the years before the Gold Glove Award, the position was dominated by players such as Yankee Phil "Scooter" Rizzuto and Brooklyn Dodger George "Pee Wee" Reese, whose nicknames say it all. Little Luis "Looie" Aparicio is thought of as the best shortstop of the 1960s. He won the Gold Glove ten times, and is the all-time leader in games played, assists and double plays.

This stereotype has changed a lot in the last 15 years. Artifical turf has made the game much quicker, forcing modern shortstops to play deeper into the outfield. This means they must be big enough to cover more ground and make longer throws. Though there are still a few short shortstops around, modern players tend to be taller. Gold Glove winners Mark Belanger, Robin Yount and Alan Trammell are all over six feet.

Ozzie "The Wiz" Smith is five-feet, 11-inches. With many strong years still ahead of him, fans are already calling Smith the greatest infielder ever to have played the game. He has won the Gold Glove Award every year since 1980, and it does not look like anybody will take it away from him.

Smith makes the toughest infield position look easy. And no matter what second baseman Frank White might say, shortstop *is* the toughest. A shortstop needs more speed, dexterity, better hands, and a stronger arm than any other infielder. Unlike first, second and third-sackers, because of the long throw a shortstop cannot

*Robin Yount can handle a bat as well as he handles a glove.*

afford to bobble the ball for a split-second. In the big leagues, a shortstop going deep in the hole to his right might have to make a 140-foot throw to first!

Also, the shortstop works with the catcher as the team's "quarterback." He is a strategist. He relays the catcher's signals to his teammates so they know what the pitcher is throwing. And he calls the base coverage in steal situations.

This is quite a change in responsibilities for a position that did not exist in the 1840s! When the shortstop—or "short fielder"—was finally added in 1845, he was a "free spirit" and could roam the ballfield at will. Sometimes he played behind the pitcher. Sometimes he positioned himself in the outfield.

By the turn of the century, the position of shortstop had gone from nonexistent to all-important. The star player of the time was a shortstop: Honus Wagner. To this day, Wagner—along with Ty Cobb and Babe Ruth—is considered a contender for the title "Greatest Player Who Ever Lived."

Kirby Puckett

# Outfielders

**The Left Fielder**

In the majors, left field has been the traditional spot for power-hitters who did not have to be expert fielders. Why? Because left fielders have a short throw to third base and to home plate. It isn't necessary to put a great arm in left field. You have to save great arms for right field instead.

It is vital to keep runners off third. One more base and a run is scored. Surprisingly, in the modern era, major league outfielders average about two chances per game, and often go entire games without making a single play.

Left fielders seldom appear in the top ten of single-season and all-time great fielding statistics. In 1961 the Gold Glove honor was changed from awarding all three outfield positions to *any* three. It became possible for three center fielders to win. And they often do.

### Fielding Trivia

*Q:* What Dodger first baseman, having played in more than 150 games, had a 1.000 FA in 1984?
*A:* Steve Garvey.

*Q:* What second baseman set a modern era single-season record for assists in 1983?
*A:* Ryne Sandberg.

*Q:* What Phillie center fielder set modern era single-season records for putouts six times in his career?
*A:* Richie Ashburn.

*Q:* What Orioles pitcher picked off three runners at first, all in one inning?
*A:* Tippy Martinez.

*Boston's Carl Yastrzemski goes after a home-run-bound ball during the 1969 All-Star game.*

In fact, the only left fielder to consistently win the Gold Glove Award through the '60s and '70s was Carl "Yaz" Yastrzemski of the Boston Red Sox. Cutting runners down with his lightning arm, Yaz led American League outfielders in assists seven times.

Today, all this is changing. Hot, ball-hawking left fielders are in abundance. Think of the explosive Rickey Henderson, Tim Raines, Bo Jackson, and Barry Bonds. Bonds' father, Bobby—who won a Gold Glove in 1973—played spectacular right field for the Giants. When father and son played ball, guess who played center? Barry's godfather and his father's center field partner: Giant Hall of Famer Willie Mays!

Left field flycatchers have one thing in common: speed. The change from grass to artificial turf has transformed big league left field play. Fleet-footed, today's left fielders play their position like wider-ranging shortstops. They cover more ground, in close or deep in the corner, fielding tricky bounces off the wall. As a result, they make more putouts and assists. Perhaps soon their names will start to appear in the top-ten putouts and assists columns.

But whether or not these players win awards on the basis of statistics is not important. They are the finest ever to have played the position. It could be that left field will be the defensive spot to watch in the '90s.

**The Center Fielder**

Who has not seen the famous film clip of Willie Mays' running over-the-head catch in the 1954 World Series? Cleveland Indian Vic Wertz's drive to deepest center seemed like a sure thing until Mays caught up with it. It could be the most famous defensive play of all time. Famous, but not the best. Mays himself made better ones. While in the minor leagues, with a runner on third and one out, Mays raced deep to his right, caught a long, hard drive with his bare right hand, and threw the runner out at the plate!

Not many would argue about Willie Mays being the greatest center fielder of all time. He invented the "basket catch," catching pop-ups and flies with his glove turned up about belt high. He is the all-time lifetime leader in putouts. He won the Gold Glove from its first year, 1957, through 1968.

Those who would argue might claim that Tris Speaker, who played from 1907 to 1928, was the

*The Catch: Willie Mays saves the game during the 1954 World Series against the Cleveland Indians.*

greatest. In the "dead ball" era, Speaker could play close in, almost like an infielder. He once made four *unassisted* double plays in one game. And then someone might say no, Ty "The Georgia Peach" Cobb, who played at the same time as Speaker, was the greatest. Or the Yankees' "Joltin'" Joe DiMaggio and Mickey Mantle. Or Brooklyn Dodger Duke Snider. Maybe Richie Ashburn of the Philadelphia Phillies.

Center field is the wide open spaces where many of baseball's heroes live—heroes who are expected to do it all. Center fielders must run the farthest and fastest to the deepest reaches of the field. They leap and snag 400-foot drives off the wall. They cover more ground and see more action. They have the longest throw to the most crucial base on the diamond: home plate. Like the catcher behind the plate, the center fielder is the communicator in the outfield.

Through the '60s and '70s, eight-time Gold Glove winner Paul Blair of the Baltimore Orioles dominated the position. Fred Lynn and Willie Wilson followed in his footsteps. During the first half of the '80s, Dale Murphy did the same. Like many center fielders, Murphy became one of the finest all-around players of the decade.

So what player are all those chattering fans watching at the moment? Kirby Puckett of the Minnesota Twins. Already a four-time Gold Glove winner, this batting champion center fielder has many people saying he is the best they have seen since Willie Mays. Puckett has robbed many a hitter of a home run by leaping high and extending his glove over the outfield fence.

**The Right Fielder**

Little league boys and girls usually think that right field is where you put the weakest fielder on the

*When a flyball goes sailing it takes the work of
Dwight Evans to haul it in.*

team. But this is the biggest myth in little league. To keep runners from scoring home, a right fielder needs a great arm—a "cannon." You don't put Dave Parker or Dave Winfield in right field for nothing!

Imagine saying that right fielders Hank Aaron and Babe Ruth played the position where the coach put the weakest players! A three-time Gold Glove winner, Aaron had an arm that base runners feared. He is sixth on the lifetime putouts list. The five players ahead of him are all center fielders.

Babe Ruth started out as a first-class pitcher and moved to center before settling into right field, where his defensive play matched his hitting. And let's not forget Yankee Roger Maris, whose record-breaking 61 homers overshadowed his superior defensive play.

Right field is the second-most important position in the outfield. A good right fielder must make the long, difficult throw to third that prevents a runner on first from advancing past second on a single. If he does not, chances are the hitter will wind up with an extra base. Right fielders are responsible for covering both first and second. Covering second on a double play ball hit to third or short is a must. Without that cover, the runner could score in the event of a bad throw to second.

When the Gold Glove rules for outfielders were changed in 1961, left fielders became all but forgotten, and right fielders filled in the spaces. The Gold Glove lists for outfielders after 1961 are heavy with two right fielders: Al Kaline of the Detroit Tigers, a ten-time winner, and the Pirates' Roberto Clemente, who captured the position from 1961 until 1972.

Roberto Clemente died tragically in a plane crash in December 1972, while bringing food and supplies to earthquake victims in Nicaragua. He was the most exciting player of the decade. His wicked line drives, blazing speed, thunderbolt arm and fearless play made him one of the most dazzling players to put on a glove.

Today, right field continues to hold its status in the big leagues as the glamor position. Players who work right field wield big bats and have rocket arms. Few players *ever* tried to stretch a base on Dwight Evans, a seven-time Gold Glove winner, in his prime. Dave Winfield, a five-time recipient, seems to stare down base runners.

So, young right fielders, take heart: you are playing one of the most wonderful positions in the game of baseball.

# Conclusion

Defense is baseball at its best. Strong pitching and tough defense can carry a weak hitting team. The wizards with the gold gloves create baseball magic. It is defense that creates the game's delightful complexity.

It is fun thinking about the game's great glovemen, but comparisons are hard. First, there is the difficulty of comparing old-time to modern-era players. In fact, it is probably impossible. The game has changed too much. Artificial turf and shifting ball park outfields have changed the game forever.

Second, literally hundreds of Gold Glove Award winners are not in this book. For nearly every name mentioned here, a dozen others could have taken their place. For every time-stopping play described, there are thousands more. That is the real beauty of defense: its variety.

Third, one element common to all great fielders is missing: practice. As youngsters, these all-stars did not wait for someone to hit them flies or grounders. They spent hours by themselves, throwing the ball high and far and running to catch it, over-the-head. Or they bounced a ball off a brick wall, learning to catch it on the short hop, making a quick return toss.

Brooks Robinson spent hours bouncing balls off his front porch. Al Kaline threw rocks at any handy target, including passing trains. Standing only a few feet away, Mike Schmidt threw golf balls at brick walls. As a boy, Ozzie Smith would lie on his back for hours, tossing a ball in the air, trying to catch it with his eyes closed.

Practice. It's what makes a player a Gold Glove winner.

# Glossary

**BLUE DARTER.** A hard-hit ground ball or low line drive that moves so fast it looks like a blue streak.

**BOOT.** An error. Fielders mishandling a play are said to have "booted" the ball away, as if they had kicked it.

**COMEBACKER.** A ground ball hit up the middle, also known as a ball hit "back through the box."

**HANDS.** Good infielders are said to have good "hands." Sometimes they are said to have hands "soft as a bird dog's mouth." Bad infielders have "hands" made of iron, or "frying pan hands."

**HOT BOX.** Third base, the position that receives a lot of "blue darters" or scorching ground balls.

**SHOESTRING CATCH.** A running catch of a fly ball made right at the tops of an outfielder's shoes.

# Bibliography

**BOOKS**

Curran, William. *Mitts*. New York: William Morrow, 1985.

Durant, John. *The Story of Baseball in Words and Pictures*. New York: Hastings House, 1973.

Falkner, David. *Nine Sides of the Diamond*. New York: Times Books/Random House, 1990.

Kaplan, Jim. *Playing the Field*. Chapel Hill: Algonquin Books of Chapel Hill, 1987.

Klein, Dave. *Great Infielders of the Major Leagues*. New York: Random House, 1972.

Peters, Alexander. *Heroes of the Major Leagues*. New York: Random House, 1967.

Ritter, Lawrence, and Donald Honig. *The 100 Greatest Baseball Players of All Time*. New York: Crown Publishers, 1986.

Thorn, John, and Pete Palmer. *Total Baseball*. New York: Warner Books, 1989.

**PERIODICALS**

Wulf, Steve. "The Big Sweep." *Sports Illustrated*, October 29, 1990:18

# Index

Aaron, Hank, 42
Aparicio, Luis, 33
Ashburn, Richie, 37, 41

Belanger, Mark, 33
Bell, Buddy, 29
Bench, Johnny, 17-18
Berra, Yogi, 17
Blair, Paul, 41
Bonds, Barry, 38
Bonds, Bobby, 38-39
Boone, Bob, 17
Boyer, Clete, 29
Boyer, Ken, 29
Brett, George, 29

Campanella, Roy, 17, 21
Carew, Rod, 25-26
Carter, Gary, 17
Chicago White Stockings, 10
Cincinnati Reds, 5, 17
Clemente, Roberto, 13, 43
Cobb, Ty, 35, 41
Collins, Eddie, 25

Dean, Dizzy, 13
DiMaggio, Joe, 31, 41

earned run average (ERA), 11
Evans, Dwight, 42, 43

fielding
    accepted chances, 10
    as defense, 6, 10-11
    assists, 11
    average (FA), 11
    judging, 10-11
    putouts, 11
Fox, Nellie, 27
Foxx, Jimmy, 23

Garvey, Steve, 37
Gehrig, Lou, 21, 23
Gibson, Bob, 13-14
Gold Glove Award, creation of, 10
Guidry, Ron, 15

Hartnett, Gabby, 17
Hatcher, Billy, 5
Henderson, Rickey, 38
Hernandez, Keith, 20, 23

Jackson, Bo, 5, 38

Kaat, Jim, 13-14
Kaline, Al, 43, 44
Kansas City Royals, 29
Kell, George, 31

Lajoie, Napolean, 10
Lynn, Fred, 41

Mantle, Mickey, 41
Maris, Roger, 43
Martin, Billy, 25
Martinez, Tippy, 37
Mattingly, Don, 23
Mays, Willie, 11, 39-40, 41
Mazeroski, Bill, 25
McDougal, Gil, 13
Murphy, Dale, 41

Nettles, Graig, 21, 29
Niekro, Phil, 15

Oakland Athletics (A's), 5-6
Ott, Mel, 9

Palmer, Jim, 15
Parker, Dave, 42
Parrish, Lance, 17
Philadelphia Phillies, 29
Puckett, Kirby, 36, 41

Raines, Tim, 38
Reese, George, 33
Reuschel, Rick, 15
Richardson, Bobby, 25, 27
Rijo, Jose, 5
Rizzuto, Phil, 33
Robinson, Brooks, 29-30, 44
Robinson, Jackie, 25
Rose, Pete, 25-28
Ruth, Babe, 35, 42

Sabo, Chris, 4-6
Sandberg, Ryne, 24, 26, 37
Santo, Ron, 29
Schmidt, Mike, 28, 29, 44
Schoendienst, Red, 27
Score, Herb, 13
Shantz, Bobby, 15
Sisler, George, 22
Smith, Ozzie, 10, 32-33, 44
Snider, Duke, 41
Speaker, Tris, 39-41
St. Louis Browns, 10

Trammel, Alan, 33
Traynor, Harold, 29
Triandos, Gus, 17

Wagner, Honus, 10, 35
White, Frank, 26-27, 33
Wilhelm, Hoyt, 17
Wilson, Hack, 8
Wilson, Willie, 41
Winfield, Dave, 42, 43

Yastrzemski, Carl, 38
Yount, Robin, 33

# About The Author

Doug Marx is a 41-year-old poet and freelance writer who, when not reading books or writing them, suffers from baseball on the brain. Having played at the Little League, high school and college levels, he now plays a hot third base for the Grass Stains, a men's softball team. Marx, who spent the better part of his childhood bouncing rubber-coated hardballs off brick walls, has also spent many years coaching boys' and girls' Little League teams. He lives in Portland, Oregon, with his wife and three children.

**Photo Credits**

ALLSPORT USA: 4, 5, 34, 42 (Otto Greule, Jr.); 18, 32 (Kirk Schlea); 20 (ALLSPORT); 22, 24, 26 (Jonathan Daniel); 36 (T. Inzerillo)
AP Wide World Photos: 16, 38, 40
Ted Astor: 6
National Baseball Library, Cooperstown, NY: 9, 14, 28, 30
UPI: 8, 12

T 38480

J 64,856
796.357
mar    Marx

Gold Gloves

Series: Baseball Heroes

**WITHDRAWN**